Dr. Snoopy's Advice to Pet Owners

By Dr. Snoopy
Illustrations by Charles M. Schulz

Andrews and McMeel
A Universal Press Syndicate Company
Kansas City

Dr. Snoopy's Advice to Pet Owners copyright © 1993 by
United Feature Syndicate, Inc. All rights reserved. Printed in
the United States of America. No part of this book may be used
or reproduced in any manner whatsoever without written
permission except in the case of reprints in the context of
reviews. For information, write Andrews and McMeel, a
Universal Press Syndicate Company, 4900 Main Street,
Kansas City, Missouri 64112.

Library of Congress Cataloging-in-Publication Data

Schulz, Charles M.
    Dr. Snoopy's advice to pet owners / by Dr. Snoopy ;
illustrations by Charles M. Schulz.
      p.   cm.
    ISBN 0-8362-4712-4 : $6.95
    1. Dogs—Humor.   2. Dogs—Caricatures and cartoons.
I. Title.
PN6727.S3Z464   1993
741.5'973—dc20   93-25379
                                                      CIP

Dear Dr. Snoopy:

My dog Frisky barks a lot when somebody comes. One time he almost ripped the gate door off. (And in case you need this information, he's half collie and half German shepherd.)

Duane Neal, Charlotte, NC

It sounds like you have a pretty ferocious dog, but he might come in handy in case you are ever attacked by a gate door.

Dear Dr. Snoopy:

My dog, Andy, always tries to talk to me and my family. He goes Owooooow! Owoowoo! Do you know what he is saying, Doctor? (He is part Border collie, part bird dog, if that will help you.)

Thomas Umberger, Metropolis, IL

I think what your dog is trying to tell you is that you are standing on his tail.

Dear Dr. Snoopy:

I had a dog named Scotter, but we had to move and my mom and dad wouldn't let us bring her. The problem is that my mom won't let me get another puppy. And every night when I think about Scotter I start to cry. Could you help me?

Jeanie Greenwell, Destrehan, LA

There is nothing wrong with crying about a lost friend. You have my sympathy. I can assure you, however, that time will help to heal this hurt, even though you will never completely forget about Scotter.

Dear Dr. Snoopy:

I know that when a dog and cat fight you have to get rid of the cat, but how about when two dogs fight? Please help.

Gary Devlin, Antioch, CA

When a dog and a cat fight, get rid of the cat. When two dogs fight, you should also get rid of the cat. See how simple it is?

Dear Dr. Snoopy:

Every night when we sit down to eat supper, my little puppy sits up and begs, and when we give him a bone, he goes and hides it in shoes. What do you suggest we do?

Tammy, Brewton, AL

I don't see where this is such a problem unless he starts to bury the bones and shoes, too. Then you have a problem. It is very difficult to get to school on time in the morning if you have to go out into the backyard and dig up your shoes.

Dear Dr. Snoopy:

I love to watch your TV shows. When Joe Cool is on, my goldfish watch him. When your show is off my gold goldfish bites my black goldfish's tail. Most of the time they get along with each other. Why does my gold goldfish do this?

Clyde Berry, Richmond, VA

I don't know anything about goldfish. I have met a few sharks in my time, and they were pretty sharp. I am glad to hear, however, that they like our shows. I wonder what they look like when seen from under water. I could try it, but I would probably drown.

Dear Dr. Snoopy

My cat Smokey meows wrong and we don't know why. Do you have any advice?

Tiffany McCumber, Mesa, AZ

I am not sure what you mean by "meowing wrong." As far as I am concerned, cats never do anything right! Who says he meows wrong? Have you discussed it with the other cats in the neighborhood?

Dear Dr. Snoopy:

I have a dachshund who wags his tail and he wags his tail on me. What should I do?

Katie Therieau, Cathedral City, CA

I would watch him very closely. If he wags his tail too much, he is liable to take off like a helicopter!

Dear Dr. Snoopy:

We bought my dog, Muffin, a nice bed, but he still sleeps on a stair that's next to the bed. And he tears the cushion from the bed into pieces. (But he is a very calm dog most of the time.) How should I get him to sleep in his bed?

Susan, Blue Island, IL

I think Muffin likes to sleep on the stairs because he is afraid of getting mugged. Lots of dogs do this, and it's not such a bad idea, as long as you don't trip on him or over him when you are going downstairs to get a drink of water. Actually, all of these problems drive me crazy. I wish that everyone had a dog as perfect as I . . .

Dear Dr. Snoopy:

I begged and begged my mom for a dog. But she won't let me get one. I wanted a dog ever since I was born. And I'll just die without one. She said I can't get one until I move away from my house. I have a hamster and she's adorable. But I'm not satisfied. What should I do?

Jennifer Quigley, Garden City, MI

I don't believe you are going to die just because you don't have a dog. People don't die from things like that. Take good care of your hamster, and maybe some day when you get your own home, you can have your own beagle.

Dear Dr. Snoopy:

I have a kitten named Tappy and she acts really strange sometimes. Like, sometimes she's so cuddly and at other times she hunches up her back like a black cat on Halloween and acts so mean when I try to come near her. What should I do?

Misty Contreras, Vidor, TX

Why does everyone write to me about cats? I don't know anything about cats. The one who lives next door to me is so ugly, you wouldn't believe it. Every time I look at him, he slashes my dog house. In regard to your cat, however, I think you are right. She is a "Halloween Cat," and they are even more weird than the rest of them!

Dear Dr. Snoopy:

My dog Tippy is afraid of cats. He always lets the cat eat his food. I am afraid that Tippy will starve to death pretty soon if he doesn't start eating. What should I do? You are the only one who can save Tippy's life.

Liza Reed, Warsaw, IN

Hurry up and start feeding Tippy in another room where the cat won't eat his food. If I were there, I would punch that stupid cat in the nose. But, of course, that's easy to say, considering I am not there.

Dear Dr. Snoopy:

My dog is a Scottish terrier named Lucia di Lammermoor. We call her Lucy for short. She's very well behaved most of the time, but she has one weakness: she loves to bark at other dogs. What should I do?

Jessica Gretch, Washington, DC

Frankly, I don't think that barking at other dogs is a weakness. Do you think that when you talk to other girls, this is a weakness? Another thought occurs to me: maybe your dog doesn't like being called "Lucy." The next time you stand out on the front steps calling for her, try using her real name. I would love to hear that!

Dear Dr. Snoopy:

My whole family are dog lovers. But I live in an apartment and there aren't any dogs allowed. I want one badly, and I don't think I'm going to move for a while.

Sharon Wilensky, Eastchester, NY

Perhaps you could volunteer to take shut-in dogs for walks. They would enjoy it, and their owners would be grateful. It would also keep you from getting mugged!

Dear Dr. Snoopy:

I have a dog named Snoopy. He is my dog but he loves my mom better. What should I do?

Joel Galassini, Albuquerque, NM

Be happy that he loves your mom. Maybe everyone loves your mom. I wouldn't doubt it. Don't worry about it.

Dear Dr. Snoopy:

My dog is four years old. When I come home after being gone for only twenty minutes she jumps on me like I've been gone for three hours. Is something wrong with her there?

Tiffany Loose, Tucson, AZ

I guess everyone gets annoyed when dogs jump on them, and I think they should learn not to do it to strangers, for it really can be irritating. I am told that if you bump a dog on the chest with your knee, this will sometimes teach the dog not to jump. Some trainers even recommend stepping on their toes, but I can tell you that really smarts, especially when you're not wearing shoes! In closing, however, please be reminded that it is nice to have someone be glad to see you when you come home, even if you have been gone only twenty minutes.

Dear Dr. Snoopy:

I have a dog whose name is Brandy. He's a Shetland sheepdog (shelty or miniature collie). We brought him to obedience school and he is very obedient. But when he is not training he bites older ladies' ankles. He would never bite anyone but they're afraid of him. I have a big problem. Please help!

Emily Richter, Harwick, VT

I thought your letter was very funny. The reason your dog bites older ladies' ankles is probably because they don't move fast enough. It's hard for me to believe that they taste any different from young ankles—but, what do I know???

Dear Dr. Snoopy:

I'm a huge fan of yours, but my dog Marcus Benjamin Lowers has a problem. He hates me. We have had him for eight years and every time I pick him up he growls. But he is so cute I wish he would like me. Help!

Amy Lowers, Parkersburg, WV

I have no idea why your dog hates you. Maybe if I could talk to him on the phone, I could find out, but I guess that wouldn't be practical. Your problem baffles me, but lately almost everything baffles me!

Dear Dr. Snoopy:

I have an Old English sheepdog named Leo. He is one year old. He is supposed to be like a watchdog, but when strange people come over he gets really excited and jumps all over them, slobbers, runs around, and cries. He is too big of a dog to be jumping and hurting people. What should I do?

Danielle Ambrose, Cleveland, OH

I agree with you that it is very annoying to have a big dog jump all over you. This is why I usually stay home. I hate being jumped on by big dogs. Old English sheepdogs also seem to want to tell you long, boring stories about how they used to watch those sheep. I hate long, boring stories. I think I would rather be jumped on!

Dear Dr. Snoopy:

My dog is a little Yorkie. He has trouble with his back legs. Every time he walks across the floor his legs give out. We took him to the vet and he said he has trick knee. His name is Puddy. Now we sometimes call him Tricky Puddy. Does that name hurt his feelings?

Molly, Delaware

The trick knee obviously came about when he played football in high school. Now that he is older, he probably will have to confine himself to things like shuffleboard. Regarding his name, I feel that it not only hurts his feelings, but probably embarrasses him terribly in front of his friends. Try changing his name to "Rex." "Rex" is a very good dog name, unless, of course, someone in your family happens to have that name already.

Dear Dr. Snoopy:

My dog digs holes, and my mom said that maybe my dog will be put in the pound. What should I do?

Kristy, Tucson, AZ

Plant trees and bushes in the holes, and your mom will never know the difference.

Dear Dr. Snoopy:

My dog doesn't seem to be eating as well as he used to. What should I do?

Kyra, Rhode Island

Try taking him to a different restaurant!

P.S. Make sure you leave the waitress a big tip, because waitresses have dogs to support, too.

Dear Dr. Snoopy:

I am going to get a dog soon. I have been begging my parents for one. I love dogs. I want to get a boy schnauzer dog. I thought of a name for him; it is Brownie. I HATE CATS AND SO DOES MY WHOLE FAMILY.

Lara Kroop, Woodbury, NJ

Your letter brought much joy to my life, although I don't think "Brownie" is such a great name. How about "Rex"? "Rex" is a great name for a dog. "Rover" is a good name, too.

Dear Dr. Snoopy:

Whenever I eat something my dog always barks like she wants something to eat, so I give her a snack and when she's done eating it she'll keep on doing it. What should I do?

David Chotiner, Northridge, CA

Tell your dog that if she eats too many snacks, she's going to have to go to an aerobics class every morning. I don't think she'll want to do that! She sounds like the kind of dog that will listen to reason. Most of us dogs are like that. We are very understanding if people explain things to us. What we don't like is yelling and screaming. Incidentally, while I was dictating this letter to Woodstock, I had another snack, and now if you will excuse me, I am off to my aerobics class . . .

Dear Dr. Snoopy:

Ever since my mom had her baby, my dog has been acting weird. What should I do?

Angie, Pennsylvania

I think your dog and the new baby need to sit down and have a long talk. Perhaps there are some misunderstandings here that you are not aware of. Try to listen in on their conversations and let me know what they have to say; then I can advise you further.

Dear Dr. Snoopy:

I have a dog named Sonny. He is afraid of almost everything; he is afraid of ducks, water, sometimes cats, and a lot of other things. What should I do?

Leanne Ng, Irvine, CA

I don't blame your dog for being afraid of ducks, water, and cats. However, he shouldn't be afraid of "other things." I wonder what "other things" are? I am not afraid of "other things," but I sure stay away from those ducks, water, and cats!

Dear Dr. Snoopy:

I need some advice on how to like dogs better. Every time a dog comes near me I run. Could you help me?

Lora Rose, Warsaw, NC

Your problem is certainly not unusual, for there are quite a few people in this world who don't like dogs. There must be at least a dozen. As you get older, you will probably lose your fear of dogs, and not run when a dog approaches. Actually, all this does is cause the dog to chase you, and the dog might even jump on you. It is much better to stand still. Just look the dog in the eye and speak firmly. Once you get over this fear of dogs, you will like them better. Then, there will only be eleven people in the world who don't like dogs!

Dear Dr. Snoopy:

I have a dog named Bambie. He was small and skinny when I bought him. Then a couple of years later he grew and got fat from eating too much. So, can you tell me how to make him lose weight, because he weighs thirteen pounds for a small Chihuahua.

Yvette Rookmaaker, Hawthorne, CA

I am not an expert on diets, but I do know that you should take your dog to your local veterinarian and have him tell you what to do. Almost all of these serious problems can be solved best simply by consulting an animal doctor.

Dear Dr. Snoopy:

Our dog Willie barks at anyone in a uniform. He terrifies the meter reader and the mailman. In fact, once he bit the mailman on the leg. What should we do?

Dan and Kent Wooldridge, Chico, CA

See if you cant find a first sergeant to come to your house in uniform. First sergeants, especially in the infantry, are very tough, and hell straighten your dog out in a hurry. Hell teach him to salute, and to march, and to do all sorts of things. Hell give your dog, Willie, a tough time. I can see it now—Poor Willie . . .

Dear Dr. Snoopy:

I'm eleven years old and I have a beagle. (You'd like her.) She's nice and cute but she's hardly ever home. She wanders all day and I hardly ever see her. We live in the country on eighty acres but she's hardly ever on them. What should I do?

Ginger, Kansas

I think it's quite possible that she goes into town to do some shopping. No one likes to stay in the country all of the time. Maybe she just enjoys wandering around bookstores and things like that. I know I do. If I ever see her I will tell her that she should stay home with you a little more. I will tell her how much you worry about her.

P.S. What does she look like?

Dear Dr. Snoopy:

My cousin's dog keeps chewing on things that aren't good for him, like big chunks of wood, telephone cords, and yesterday, we saw him chewing on the house. He is not a puppy so we know he is not teething. Then we thought he just might like to chew on things so we bought him some rawhide bones, and he still does it. For his sake, I hope you can help him, because we don't know why he is doing this, and he is really getting himself into trouble!

Cheri Tawney, San Jose, CA

I think your dog is simply bored. Dogs chew on things and dig holes in the garden because they have nothing else to do. I suppose you could get him a library card, but then, he would sit around all day reading, and you wouldn't like that either. I admit, you have a real problem here. Maybe you could chew on the side of his dog house and see how he likes it! 49

Dear Dr. Snoopy:

Our dog just had five brand-new puppies. Do you have any suggestions for names?

Harvey, Louisiana

I have always liked the name "George." Why not name them "George the 1st, George the 2nd, George the 3rd, George the 4th, and George the 5th . . ."

Dear Dr. Snoopy:

I have a German shepherd named Cleo. Every time I'm eating something, she always wants some. When I give her some she always bites my fingers to get it. One time I was going fishing and I couldn't find any worms so I used a hot dog. I caught a fish, and had a piece of hot dog on the hook and she tried to eat it, but she got the hook stuck in her nose. What should I do?

Mike McGrath, Fremont, OH

One of the reasons that dogs sometimes bite your fingers when you are handing us something is our tendency to pull away quickly, which causes us to snatch at whatever you are giving us. Start with larger objects and hold your hand perfectly still. This eventually will teach Cleo that she doesn't have to leap frantically to get the object before you drop it or pull it away.

Dear Dr. Snoopy:

Most every night my dog named Tiffany jumps on my bed and lays on my feet and if I move she'll bite me. Do you have any good advice?

Eric Lancaster, El Cajon, CA

Try sleeping in the upper bunk. Either that, or wear your army boots to bed—or your hockey skates. I have never seen a dog yet that could bite your feet when you are wearing hockey skates.

Dear Dr. Snoopy:

When I take my dog to the lake, I can't seem to get him to swim out after sticks that I throw in the water. What do you suggest?

Luke Lombardi, Kansas City, MO

I suggest that you let him throw the sticks, and you swim out to get them. That'll teach both of you a lesson!

Dear Dr. Snoopy:

I know you have been to France. If you don't mind, tell me what to expect. I am an exchange student and I will stay for three weeks at a French girl's home. I am quite nervous, although I know some French. Please help me!

Ryan Henderson, Michigan Center, MI

Well, for one thing, don't expect too much. You will enjoy the restaurants, but you should be careful not to eat too much rich food. I learned that the hard way when I would visit Paris on furlough. I remember taking this one cute little French lass out to dinner this one particular night, but no, the memories are too harsh. I would rather not think about it. Anyhow, I hope you have a good time.

Dear Dr. Snoopy:

I have a problem. My dog Snuffy always digs holes under the fence to see the dogs next door. How can I break her of this habit?

David Lester, Phoenix, AZ

Well, I suppose you could put some larger rocks along the fence where Snuffy digs, but maybe if you had a great big dog party some day, Snuffy wouldn't feel she had to go next door. You could invite all the dogs over and serve them chocolate chip cookies and root beer. If you decide to do this, let me know, because I might want to be there. I might even bring Spike along. He loves parties, and they never seem to have any where he lives.

Dear Dr. Snoopy:

Our dog doesn't seem to be a very good watchdog. What can we do about this?

Mike Camacho, Tampa, FL

I once knew some people who owned a St. Bernard. If the St. Bernard sleeps by the front door, there is always the chance that a burglar might trip over him in the dark. If your dog is a smaller type, you could always throw him at an intruder. Teaching your dog to bark loudly, of course, is a big help, unless the barking annoys the cat next door, which means you are all in a lot of trouble!

Dear Dr. Snoopy:

Our family has a two-year-old schnauzer named Toby. We have been keeping him warm by putting his sweaters on him for the last three weeks. All he's done since then is sleep and eat. We thought he was sick. My aunt suggested we take off his sweater and see if that would help. As soon as we took off his sweater, he started running around and playing. We decided he must have been embarrassed in his sweaters. Have you ever heard of such a thing?

Allison Hughes, Orland Park, IL

Oh yes, most of the embarrassing sweaters were ones that I received either for Christmas or on my birthday. Actually, my favorite sweaters are beagleneck sweaters.

Dear Dr. Snoopy:

I have a pet dog. He sleeps in the day and barks in the night. I wish he would do the opposite. One night I looked out of my bedroom window and saw him barking at everything that moved about him. Then I thought I should get him a doggie biscuit. So I went and got him one. That suited him for a little bit. Then he started barking again. What else should I do, Snoopy?

Karen Jennings, Red Oak, OK

Maybe if you bought him his own TV, he would stay up so late at night that he would sleep better. I don't think, however, you should spoil him by giving him all those doggie biscuits. Pretty soon, he will think you are rewarding him for barking. We dogs can get spoiled very quickly. Now, take my brother, Spike, for instance. No, on second thought, you had better not—he's weird!

Dear Dr. Snoopy:

My dog won't stop licking me. She wakes me up in the morning by licking my face. What should I do? It's gross!

Jennifer, Missouri

Perhaps you should look at yourself in the mirror. I have the feeling that you still have some grape jelly left on your face from the jelly-bread you had last night just before you went to bed.

Dear Dr. Snoopy:

I want a dog very badly. My grandfather has a dog and I have a rabbit. I love them both, but the rabbit doesn't play and my grandfather never lets me walk or play with his dog. I want my own dog so that I can play with it and walk it whenever I want to. How can I convince my parents (my father mostly) that we desperately NEED a dog?

Molly Norman, Lyons, IL

Why don't you go for a walk with your grandfather? He can take his dog along and the three of you can go to the shopping mall and buy ice cream cones, and then walk around the lake. You can push him on the swing, too. (Not the dog—your grandfather.)

Dear Dr. Snoopy:

What sort of work should my dog be expected to do around the house?

Janet Hanson, Urbana, IL

Washing dishes is out! It is very uncomfortable to get your paws wet. Vacuuming is not bad, although the noise can be hard on sensitive ears. I think the best job for a dog is simply being there to greet you when you come home from school. Jumping up and down is hard work, but most dogs can do it if they are allowed plenty of rest afterward.

Dear Dr. Snoopy:

For my birthday, I am going to get a puppy, and I want to send it to obedience school. At what age should I send it?

Denise Vivancos, Hialeah, FL

I don't know, how old are you?

Dear Dr. Snoopy:

I have a dog named Tippy. She's always wanting to play ball. But the ball is all slobbery. What should I do? Do you think I could sign her up for baseball? Her age group uses a soft nylon ball. She'd be good use on Charlie Brown's team.

Frank Lynn, Merced, CA

I think your idea for playing baseball with Tippy is a good one. The question is, will she like playing on grass or on Astroturf? Also, who are you going to get to sing the National Anthem before your game begins? Will she want a three-year contract, and what position will she play? These are things you have to think about.

Dear Dr. Snoopy:

I have a dog named Tiny. Every time he sees another person outside, he starts to bark, but when they come up to Tiny and start petting and kissing him, Tiny starts licking them too. When someone comes near his bed or dog dish, he charges after them and bites them. My dad tried to stop him from doing this, but Tiny just keeps on. Have you any advice?

Sandy Peterson, Lincoln, IL

I don't see anything wrong with the way your dog has been acting. If anyone came near my dog dish, I would bite him too. The part in your letter that confuses me is where you tell about people kissing your dog. You must have strange friends!

Dear Dr. Snoopy:

My dog has a serious problem. She plays with cats and I actually think she likes them. One time she almost climbed a tree after a cat. I think she might turn into a cat one day. What should I do?

Monica Lopes, Burnet, TX

This is the most frightening problem I have ever heard. I cannot think of anything worse than having a dog turn into a cat! Actually, however, there is nothing wrong with dogs and cats playing together. I, personally, would never get involved with anything that foolish, but I try to be broad-minded. If your dog does turn into a cat some day, call the newspaper and let them know. Maybe they will put you and your dog/cat on TV, and you will become rich and famous!

Dear Dr. Snoopy:

I have two cats. One of my cats tends to be hyper. We were staying at a friend's house and he did about 500 dollers damige. What should I do?

Dereth, Ojai, CA

The first thing you should do is learn how to spell "dollars," "damage," and "should." After that, I guess you are just going to have to get a job and pay for the "damige" with the "dollers" you earn.

Dear Dr. Snoopy:

I have a dog named Lady and two cats. She always wants to play with them or try to make them friends but my cats don't want to make friends or play. All they want to do is be lazy and hungry. Sometimes Lady gets scratched by them. Well you see I'm an animal lover, but I'd like to spank both of the cats for Lady, but I can't! What should I do?

Trudy Scott, Cubero, NM

If I get one more letter about cats, I think I'll lose my mind! What I need is a good crocodile letter.

Dear Dr. Snoopy:

My dog is white and you can see him very easily in the dark when you go out. However, our other dog is jet black and underfoot. We can't see him at all at night and we trip over him. Please help!

Chris Knorr, Millington, MI

The answer is absurdly simple. Put your dog outside when it's snowing.

Dear Dr. Snoopy:

I have a bigger problem than last time. We have a new dog and his name is Popeye. You would think maybe that he is a good dog, but he's not. He is a real pain. He'll sit outside in the backyard and cry and bark and cry and so on. And we always have to keep going back and forth to tell him to be quiet. What should we do?

Jennifer Pappas, Mission Hills, CA

I find it difficult to believe that you don't understand the loneliness of your dog. No one likes to sit outside all by himself with nothing to do. He needs companionship. Take him into town and show him how to play video games.

Dear Dr. Snoopy:

My mom wants to get two kittens so they can play with each other. But my dad says that we can only get one. If we only get one kitten, she will be very lonely with no one to play with, except for our mean poodle named Buffy. What do you think we should do?

Becky Rootes, Zimmerman, MN

Lots of people have only one kitten, and that kitten doesn't become lonely. If you had two kittens, maybe they would become lonely because you don't have three kittens. If you think about it, where could all this end? But, don't think about it . . .

Dear Dr. Snoopy:

My dog keeps biting me. I really would like him to stop because there soon won't be anything left of me. What should I do?

Janelle Phillips, Overland Park, KS

Explain to him very carefully that biting, in most cases, is morally wrong. In some ancient cultures, it might be permitted or even encouraged, but I have found that all it does these days is get you into trouble. My advice, of course, applies not only to your dog, but to any brothers or sisters you might have.

P.S. It could also apply to aunts and uncles.

Dear Dr. Snoopy:

I want to keep my dog's teeth sweet and clean. Can I brush her teeth and do I use powder or paste?

Lena, Burlingame, CA

I think the hard part is going to be teaching your dog how to hold onto the toothbrush. Also, does she have any trouble standing on the stool to reach the sink? This leads us to other problems such as taking a shower. Should you let her do it in the morning or at night before she goes to bed? I don't know. This is too much for me to think about!

Dear Dr. Snoopy:

My dog looks just like you except he's fat. How do you stay so skinny?

Andrea Gardea, Stockton, CA

If you think I'm skinny, you should see my brother, Spike. He lives out in the desert all by himself, and I am sure all he ever eats are TV dinners. I often wonder where he cooks them, because I don't think he has a microwave. Anyhow, don't let your dog get too fat because it isn't good for him.

Dear Dr. Snoopy:

I have a cat that barks! What should I do?

Allison, Rego Park, NY

Don't do anything. Let him or her bark. Barking is the best thing that anyone can do. It is meowing that gets you into trouble.

Dear Dr. Snoopy:

My dog acts like a hog. Every time pots and pans rattle he is underfoot. When we sit down to eat he barks and whines while we eat. What should we do to break him of the habit?

Callie Chapman, Lawton, OK

I find it impossible to answer a question that was written to me on a piece of "Garfield" stationery.

Dear Dr. Snoopy:

My cat Cindy takes most of the day to eat her tuna, so Tommy, our setter, has been helping himself. Now Cindy has taken to stealing from Tommy's dish. What can I do?

Hilary, Glen Ellen, CA

We have been getting a lot of letters from dog and cat owners who have pets who eat each other's food. Perhaps we have here what is called a failure to communicate. It is very important that your kitchen menus be written clearly so that each pet knows what he is ordering. I would not recommend menus in French because there are still a few dogs and cats around who have difficulty with foreign language menus.

Dear Dr. Snoopy:

I begged my mom to have a dog. But she hates dogs. But everybody else loves dogs. What should I do?

Jamie, Paterson, NJ

I can't believe that your mom really hates dogs. If I could just sit down and talk with her for a few hours, I am sure that I could charm her socks off! Of course, I can't, so that puts us right back where we started. I guess you have a real problem.

Dear Dr. Snoopy:

I have a dog named Pokey. He is a white West Highland terrier and our neighbors, "the Trainers," have a golden retriever named Sunny. He's nice to people but not to other dogs. He's always in our yard and it's not fair to Pokey so he can't come out even in his own yard but if we yell at Sunny, Pokey will get defensive and start a big fight. Pokey has a girlfriend named Molly. She's a bulldog. Molly is my best friend Maris's dog and Sunny is mean to her too.

Chrisy DuRall, Indianapolis, IN

Your letter is too complicated. Just reading it through once has made me dizzy. I hate to get involved in neighborhood squabbles. Please don't write me any more letters that make me dizzy!

Dear Dr. Snoopy:

I am having problems with my two dogs. Every morning when my dogs are outside and the garbageman comes my dogs bark up a storm. I tell them to stop but they ignore me. What should I do to stop them from barking? I know the garbageman must hate being barked at.

Chip Hester, Baton Rouge, LA

Your biggest problem seems to be that if your dogs always bark up a storm, how can you stand living where it rains so much? Ha ha ha ha ha ha ha ha ha ha ha ha ha ha ha ha—just some more humor there to keep things going . . .

Dear Dr. Snoopy:

My dog's name is Bonnie. The problem with her is that when we feed her sometimes she takes off with the pans and never brings them back. One time my brother Jason found one under some leaves. What should we do to keep her from taking the pans?

Robin Ferguson, Lyon Co., KY

Don't do anything. If this is the only joy she has in life, why not let her be happy? As my Aunt Marion used to say, "What are a few pans between friends?" At least, I think that's what she used to say.

Dear Dr. Snoopy:

I like being a part of your fan club. It's fun. I like reading all about you to my parents, but my father says he doesn't believe that you've been to the moon, you can type, you can talk, you can read, and I don't know what to do to make him believe.

Polly White, Gloster, MS

Your father is right, and your father is wrong. I've been to the moon, obviously I can type, and I can read; but, unfortunately, I cannot talk, but who cares—dogs don't have to talk. All talking does is get you into trouble.